D0521916

St Kilda

A portrait of Britain's remotest island landscape

Photographs © Colin Baxter, 1988
Text © Jim Crumley, 1988

All rights reserved. No part of this publication may be reproduced, stored in a retrieval system, or transmitted in any form or by any means, electronic, mechanical, photocopying, recording, or otherwise without the prior permission of Colin Baxter Photography Limited.

Published by Colin Baxter Photography Ltd,
Lamington, Biggar, Lanarkshire ML12 6HW

British Library Cataloguing in Publication Data
Baxter, Colin
    St Kilda: a portrait of Britain's remotest island landscape.
    1. Scotland. Western Isles. St Kilda
    I. Title   II. Crumley, Jim
    941.1'4
ISBN 0-948661-03-8

Printed in Great Britain by Frank Peters (Printers) Ltd, Kendal

St Kilda

A portrait of Britain's remotest island landscape

Photographs by Colin Baxter

Text by Jim Crumley

Colin Baxter Photography Ltd, Lamington

Acknowledgement

St Kilda is owned by the National Trust for Scotland on behalf of the Nation and leased to the Nature Conservancy Council who manage it as one of a series of National Nature Reserves. A small part of Hirta is sub-leased to the Ministry of Defence.

The authors and publishers wish to acknowledge the kind co-operation of the National Trust for Scotland, the Nature Conservancy Council and the Ministry of Defence; without it this book would not have been possible.

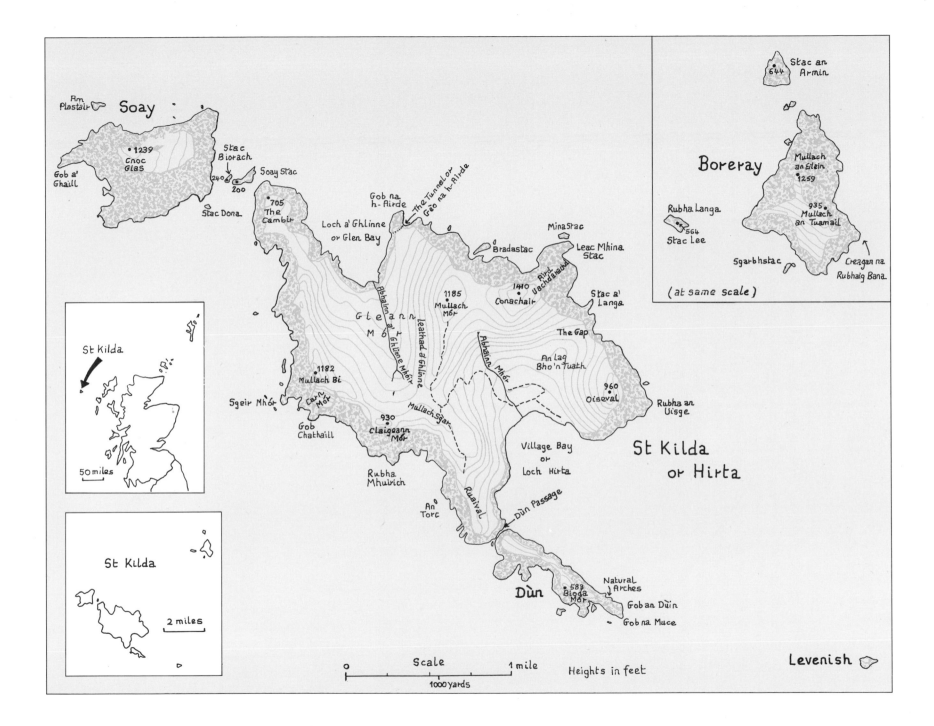

Soay

Am Plastair

· 1239
Cnoc Glas

Gob a' Ghaill

Stac Biorach

240
200

Soay Stac

Stac Dona

· 705
The Cambir

Gob na h-Airde

The Tunnel or Geo na h-Airde

Loch a' Ghlinne or Glen Bay

Mina Stac

· Bradastac

Leac Mhina Stac

Aird Uachdarachd

· 1185
Mullach Mòr

· 1410
Conachair

Stac a' Langa

Gleann Mòr

Leathad a' Ghlinne

Abhainn a' Ghlinne Mhòir

The Gap

An Lag Bho'n Tuath

· 1182
Mullach Bì

Sgeir Mhòr

Carn Mòr

Abhainn Mhòr

· 960
Oiseval

Rubha an Uisge

Gob Chathaill

· 930
Claigeann Mòr

Mullach Sgar

Village Bay
or
Loch Hirta

St Kilda
or Hirta

Rubha Mhuirich

Ruaival

An Torc

Dùn Passage

Dùn

· 583
Bioda Mòr

Natural Arches

Gob an Dùin

Gob na Muce

Levenish

Scale

0   Scale   1 mile

1000 yards

Heights in feet

Boreray

· 644
Stac an Armin

Mullach an Eilein
· 1259

Rubha Langa

· 564
Stac Lee

· 935
Mullach an Tuamail

Sgarbhstac

Creagan na Rubhaig Bana

(at same scale)

St Kilda

50 miles

St Kilda

2 miles

S T KILDA is this: it is a mad, imperfect God's hoard of all the unnecessary lavish landscape luxuries he ever devised in his madness. These he has scattered at random in Atlantic isolation 100 miles from the corrupting influences of the mainland, 40 miles west of the westmost Western Isles. He has kept for himself only the best pieces, and woven around them a plot as evidence of his madness. First he has wreathed his hoard in mists to intrigue the corrupted world, then set the lure of inaccessibility to snare its curiosity. The encompassing seas are both defender and in their own good time exquisite destroyer of St Kilda, so that it submits stubbornly and gloriously like bracken in autumn. When the seas win over and St Kilda is smoothed into the floor of the ocean as sand, the world will mourn and learn by St Kilda's example to cherish the wild places of the earth.

He has set two further lures, this God of Wilderness, to compound his plot. One is the forlorn decline and fall of the St Kildan people, culminating in the evacuation of 1930, so that the roofless homes they left behind and all the other artefacts of their civilisation stand as mute testimony to both their own artless building skills and nature's heartless way with the community – any community – once it strays towards the brink of extinction. The second is that seabirds have learned the blatant art of St Kildan survival so well that their spectacle almost rivals the landscape. These too have their lure, and as they were the St Kildans' staple diet, they also stand as a rare flourish of prey which has outlived predator.

It is to the landscape itself, however, that the St Kilda voyager is drawn again and again, rich beyond all the dreams and dire warnings, illustrations and eulogies you will ever encounter. You may study these and believe, but you must go and stand and stare to be convinced. The forcefulness of the convincing is an awesome manifestation of the power of landscape, yet so well has this God done his work that none of it is higher than 1400 feet.

There is a central island – Hirta – for a crown, with a cluster of satellite stacs and smaller islands for jewels, an eager sea for a setting, an ocean's light and winds to set it off to best effect; scale and deception on the grand scale are its stock in trade.

Yet – and here is the mad God's one imperfection – it is not an unsullied hoard he has gathered, and you must turn many blind eyes, for the mainland has touched even here and left its mark. An Army camp cheek-by-jowls it with the

The cliffs of Hırta and Soay from the east: "The encompassing seas are both defender and exquisite destroyer . . ."

old village, and a road has been flung to hilltop installations: a radar station and a missile tracking station. The imposition of these on St Kilda of all places is frankly grim, yet the Army supplies power, communications, transport, medical facilities, and keeps the islands in touch with the world which it seems they cannot now do without. Now, however, that same world which was St Kilda's downfall in many ways, has recognised the uniqueness of the place and designated it accordingly. The World Heritage Convention of UNESCO, 1987 pronounced:

> *Through the collective recognition of the community of nations expressed within the principles of the convention concerning protection of the world cultural and natural heritage, the St Kilda Archipelago of the National Trust for Scotland has been designated a World Heritage Site and joins a select list of protected areas around the world whose outstanding natural and cultural resources form the common inheritance of all mankind.*

That implies a commitment to live up to a God's standards. We may always fall short, but for as long as St Kilda is spared by her seas, we must offer the treasure store our best guardianship.

This book tells how it was for two pairs of eyes going west, looking thoughtfully, relishing wildness, respecting the past, questioning the present, and pondering the future. May it urge your own voyage westward, or if you have already voyaged, may it ease the passage of memory and compel new thoughts.

The bold sweep of Village Bay with the ragged breakwater of Dùn beyond

Here Are Not Islands

Here are not islands but an ocean's splintered toys,
frogs in the throat of the storm.

Here were not natives but futile fighting frontiersmen. The
four thousand years of their occupation was a meagre war
to wage against eternal seas.

Men's resistance here has been bettered by mice, their
best-laid schemes agley in the conspiracies of nature's
worst; their ideals and idylls overwhelmed by the high tides
of civilised curiosity.

Birds rule now – fulmar, puffin, gannet, a raucous, showy
regime with muscly bonxies for firepower – but theirs too
is no more than a long and dwindling lease of the ocean's
sufferance.

The ocean is invincible here and will prevail in time
over all their tiered might when even the cliffs
are extinct.

Here are not islands, not rocks, but seabed sands of time
to come.

ST KILDA should be greeted from the sea, from a berserk deck burrowing blindly west into oceans of winds, deserts of waves the size of dunes. There should be a mist the colour of asparagus soup and just as penetrable. There should be one wave to lift you higher than the rest and from its falling crow's nest you will glimpse sudden land, or at least land after a fashion.

In minutes its advance will baulk horizons and imaginations with its ocean-aura, its scale monstrously magnified by mists. The bottom third of a cliff – you do not yet know that it is only the bottom third – thermals up to unguessable dimensions, its spectacle compounded by the new prospect of a second cliff clearly unrelated to the first, the water threading between them violent and green and punctuated by the exclamation marks of stacs and rocks, and birds – suddenly clamoursome – by the uncountable thousand. In this light, it is the least plausible place on earth, assuming that the voyage from the Western Isles has not already convinced you that there is no longer any such place as earth.

Then, with this final savage insult to injuries of the stomach and pride, and with your mind numbed by the unfettered elemental rawness of the place, the boat swings in past Dùn, St Kilda's wildly improbable bulwark against prevailing westerlies, and in to the storm-starved Village Bay. The instant becalming is just one more giddying sensation which you hardly dare to believe.

Or perhaps you are one of the lucky ones. A gentle swell has eased sleep and you greet a pastel sunrise of grey, pink, lilac, yellow, become so engrossed in its soft eastern spell that you fail to notice a small ragged shadow hardening on the western horizon. Then a darkening of the swell commands your glance for'd and you catch the impossible profile of Boreray. You race to the bow and confront the bulkier deeper shadow of Hirta, the rock stutters of Levenish, Stac Lee and the bluntly ominous Soay. Slowly the shadows materialise, bare the detail of their preposterous architecture, sit on their waters as sculptures on pedestals.

St Kilda has seduced you before you have so much as tested her embrace. You have in common with the unlucky ones only the sensation that it is the least plausible place on earth.

However fond or foul your greeting, the St Kilda landscape commands from the first moment of your first horizon awareness with its assembly of extravagant rock gestures: towering serrations which even the most benign flat-calming sea can never quite drain of a dire aspect. These of all islands have won as many vile

"Dùn sets a vivid precedent. It is the boldest breakwater any ocean haven could wish for . . ."

oaths as paeans of praise but none of them prepares the path eternally west for what lies in wait.

Superlatives quarrel in your mind while you grapple with the first flood of sensations, and the discovery that the landscape arrogance is an almost two-dimensional bluff does nothing to devalue the superlatives, but only heightens astonishments.

The Dùn sets a vivid precedent. It is the boldest breakwater any ocean haven could wish for from the west, an eagle head with far-flung wings from the east across the bay it harbours. Yet from north and south it is a wafer of rock, as slender and frayed as an eagle wing in moult, holed and hollowed, caved and calloused by seas quite capable in their dismissive ire of throwing careless spray 600 feet into the air, drenching the summit of Dùn and falling into Village Bay beyond as salt rain. Even if you decline to see it as an eagle, and only as a withered rock, then surely some imponderable force has pushed the whole mass on its side?

The Dùn is the whittle-work of the art of sea sculptings such as these and, as such, a thing of some compelling grandeur. It was the adorning masterpiece of the St Kildans' workaday rock drapery, the backcloth of the first questing cameras, the first and last symbolic profile of the St Kilda voyager. Your first rounding of its seaward prow into Village Bay confirms the arrival, the safe haven; then as you bless or curse your wilderness God or Devil, a new St Kilda sensation steals across the deck.

The proposition that this sea-besieged citadel was once home dawns slowly; that the long wild hours behind you, wild such as you never contemplated, were once the ritual of homecoming for St Kildans on their rare journeys to Skye or the Western Isles. Hearts would long for these rocks for their beckoning familiarity, not for the challenge of their angrily jealous isolation. St Kilda was not remote to them, but everywhere else was. It is a simplistic truth, perhaps, and one which is quite outwith the compass of our own understanding, for although St Kilda is inhabited today by a few soldiers and technicians and scientists, by no definition of the term can it be considered lived in. It is a recurrent theme in any consideration of today's St Kilda.

Isolation was the safeguard which nurtured the St Kildan race and the way of life whose remnants we stroll among, and about which we still know so little.

". . . it is the least plausible place on earth . . ."

Isolation was also the challenge to the curiosity and the technology of our own race; ours was the drawing noose which strangled the St Kildans.

It is as well, perhaps, that the St Kildans did not survive into the helicopter era, but St Kilda from the air is also a valid greeting, so that the islands have a puny scale, so that they are grit in the eye of the Atlantic. It is that glimpse of St Kilda from high, from afar, which puts them as islands into nature's perspective, which makes any close-quartered familiarity with them the richer, and gives us the one understanding of St Kilda which the St Kildans never knew.

St Kilda is a world of three elements: rock, sea, seabirds. However long you stay, however passionately you revere or revile it, whether you marvel or mourn away the days, all your lasting emotions for the place cling for their sustenance to the fusion and the conflicts of that trilogy of fundamentals. The rock — volcanic, almost none of it glacial — is the spat fragments of a miles-wide crater bearing no shred of resemblance to the popular conception of a volcano. It piles and crumples into landforms, weathers and withers over aeons to satiate the island-hunger of the restless salt jaws below, whose gnawing greed is a visible everyday phenomenon.

The rock also litters Village Bay and the hills around (and drops older hints in Glen Bay across the island) in the strewn guise of the St Kildans' own memorials — the cottages, black houses, beehive houses, souterrain, cleits, dykes, fanks and folds. These spin a coarse web, a gruff charm around the bay, so that you cannot linger there for long without falling prey to the futile, fatuous and endlessly fascinating variations on the theme of "if only . . . ."

The sea has already eroded its significance into the headlands of your mind. You have learned that St Kilda is not of land as you know it but an upstart, a dying survivor of the sea. Shores have been ground into bays. Cliffs have been burrowed and slashed, peninsulas severed into islands and stacs, hills gouged from behind. The sea here is artist, architect, demolitioner, God and Devil. It is also fickle, conjuring storms from calms as readily as a conjurer plucks rabbits from an empty hat, confounding painted ships on painted oceans with unheralded hurricanes. There was no shade of St Kildan life uncoloured by the sea. It provided, it destroyed — life and limb as well as shore and stac. The school register on the teacher's desk in the village bears witness: in the column marked "reason for absence" entries like "illness" or "left the island" or "helping

"The rock litters Village Bay and the hills around in the strewn guise of the St Kildans' own memorials . . ."

17

to build the new pier" sit uneasily tabulated above and below the dark interjections of "drowned". The St Kildan's ultimate test of manhood was his abilities as a cragsman. Inability or trying too hard to impress were short-lived failings.

The sea is also a duplicitous collaborator, as trustworthy as a Judas in its conspiracies with its perpetual victim the rock to create a climate of infuriating quicksilver shifts of mood, rarely without grandeur. The collaborators brew mists, and these too service the cause of a conspiracy of many beauties, although in winter, the sea can girn at the rock for a month at a time so that Conachair weeps mist down to its waist, and wan, curt days offer little respite from months of night.

Seabirds drench St Kilda. On Hirta, the fulmars are an omnipresence, roosting douce as doves on the turfed roofs of the cleits in the village, gatecrashing your thoughtful progress along that most melancholy of grass streets, taking your silhouette by storm on the dizzy rim of the Gap where they cram every nook and cranny and impossible stances which are neither nook nor cranny, every available and some unavailable inches of every foot of 1000 feet of cliffs. That suddenness of fulmars throws you, its sound haunts you in waves. There is nowhere on St Kilda which is immune from fulmars, even in the bonxie glen, Gleann Mór, where they have taken to nesting deep inside cleits to thwart the bonxies' natural aggression. Thousands nest on the cliffs of Conachair, St Kilda's highest summit; one nests on a window ledge by the Sergeants' Mess on the shore. They are as limitless and as unfussy as that. The fulmar can be the seabirds' ambassador for now: others might fill the role better – the pet shop appeal of puffins, the brilliant blizzards of gannet luftwaffes, the Chaplinesque guillemots and razorbills (ambassadors to their coat tails), the articulate beauty of the kittiwakes – but of all these, only the fulmars sally forth to greet you. It is true that if you push a nesting bird too far it will just as soon spew evilly at you as sit pretty or dip a flypast wing, but in that the fulmar is nothing more than characteristic of its parent island.

There are other lesser elements in the sum of St Kilda's component parts, and some of these are accorded their place as this exploration treks its singular landscape, but these three fundamentals of rock, sea, seabirds, these are its primary colours, and from them are fashioned all St Kilda's shades.

Rock moods of St Kilda:

above *Sea and mists savage Soay Stac*

right *Early sun floods the cliffs of Oiseval*

IT SHOULD begin gently, or at least as gently as St Kilda will permit, for it is an arduous place for muscles and sensibilities, and takes surprising toll of both. If you have time to linger, and if you can resist its forlorn appeal, leave the village alone for a few days, because you cannot begin to understand the St Kildans without first beginning to understand their landscape.

The landscape conditioned everything — the peculiar nature of their own evolution, physically, psychologically, perhaps even spiritually; the way they hunted, the way they built; the nature of the challenge which the rest of us came to find irresistible; even the nature of the weather, for this landscape makes its own.

There are no short miles on St Kilda, and no easy prizes. For all the modest scale of the hills they all begin at sea level and climb either steeply or impossibly. Mostly the hills have no "other sides", only sea cliffs, so that the view of the hills around Village Bay, for example, is a stupendous sham, a masterly St Kilda deception, a brilliant bluff. Only by crossing north-west into Gleann Mór can you have anything like a hill walk as most people would translate the expression. Otherwise, you climb, not to a hilltop but to a clifftop. To follow the course of fulmar or gannet to the sea from one of these, or to home in on the dwindling wheeling tiers of birds for a thousand feet is to be made head-spinningly and uncompromisingly aware of St Kilda's vertical scale. That is why it should begin gently.

The Gap is a good place to begin. It is not a gap at all, but the head of a corrie with no back to it. The climb from Village Bay is modest by St Kilda's standards, but the essence of St Kilda is immediate, pungent and heady.

You climb amid the simplistically brilliant architecture of the cleits, stone-and-turf storage chambers for seabirds – the St Kildans' daily bread – and other necessities of mid-Atlantic life. They built cleits all over the island, and even on Boreray; some in the most bizarre locations imaginable, some whose locations are as unimaginable as their purpose. Their genius is in a design which sets nature to work, persuades nature to outwit itself, and serve the purpose of man in the process. In that respect, the cleits are a unique achievement, for nature is not easily outwitted on St Kilda.

Four sheep fanks – or cultivation enclosures, possibly both – lie in the lap of the hill, thoughtfully sited, unerringly built with a lack of respect for

The stupendous flank of Conachair from the Gap: ". . . the hills have no 'other sides' . . ."

Sheep Folds: An Lag Bho'n Tuath

Whose geometries were these,
whose manhandling eye
accorded every stone its place
and every line its uncouth rhyme
an unrefined stone poem?

These frames of mind
uncluttered by rigidities
of round and square
made rude amends
by hoarding stones the size
of shepherds to their bidding,
and these, worked well, land-sure,
were true enough.

The four sheep folds
stand sheepless now
but gathered by
their shepherding hills
they tend their careful flock
of teeming stones.

Such men who wrought
such shapes upon the land
are sorely missed: St Kilda
craves again the rock-sure clasp
of such ungeometric hands.

conventional shapes which accords the stonework an almost pliable air. The St Kildans' skill with stone is evident everywhere, but they built to rude rather than beautiful effect, their dykes rarely straight or circular, as these four fanks testify. One of the four is itself in four sections without a single geometrically identifiable shape among them.

The villagers built with what was to hand, so that you have to look to incomers and late comers and their influences for buildings which do not echo the natives' instinctive sympathy with their land.

There is an ambience around the fanks with at least the illusion of circling hills, the satisfying landscape aesthetic of the single curve of Village Bay and Oiseval, and the hypnotic silhouette of Dùn beyond, all of which seems somehow to have stored best the St Kilda of the St Kildans. It is not something which is easy to explain, and it is not as simple as shuttering the army camp from view, for your mind soon learns to do that as the landscape exerts its own influences. Perhaps it is nothing more than the evidence of the St Kildans' artless art and its unfailing sense of place. Prospects behind and below are so compelling that the Gap, when you reach it, comes not so much as a shock to the system as an unwillingness to believe your eyes. The map warns you that it all exists, the edge-of-the-world cliffs, the seaward miles to Boreray and its stacs, but there seems no good reason to believe it, and certainly no reason at all to believe it could all look like this.

Three things happen at the Gap to dislocate sensibilities. The first is that your hill-girt world which has wrapped the climb in well-rounded heathery securities (dash of merlin, monotone of snipe, underfoot glimmer of orchids) suddenly stops. One stride you are on the last pull up a hillside like any other, the next there is no hill left, and the stride after that would leave you in some turmoil 600 feet above the sea with no land beneath your feet. The Oiseval cliffs loom 300 feet higher to your right, the Conachair cliffs 600 feet higher to your left. Below, there are only infinite depths of birds.

The second happening is that you step into one of St Kilda's bird-climates. Fulmars are all around the village, but not like this. Here they wheel around your head, fly past side-headed, hang on the air in long black-eyed scrutinies a handful of feet away, or shake their wings like a garden sieve just above and behind your head so that you spin in expectation of some fearsome unsuspected

top *Boreray and Stacs from the Gap: ". . . not so much a shock to the system as an unwillingness to believe your eyes . . ."*

bottom *". . . the well-rounded heathery securities . . ." of the approach to the Gap*

force and find only the unblinking black eye, the sleek head, the side-slipping grace of fulmar flight. The fulmars nest here in thousands, swarm on stacs and cliff faces and grass ledges and impossible non-ledges, fill the air from clifftop to wavetop. The sitting birds bicker constantly so that there is a vast fractured sound on the cliffs, but the flying birds are utterly silent so that there is an eerie cordon about you, an unbreachable protective shield fashioned from their long looks and their soundless fearlessness.

This capacity of birds, and particularly seabirds, to so dominate hours and places around St Kilda will be one of the abiding memories. They come at you in tides, or stifle the seaward view with their strength in numbers, and muster the one force which can be equal in its visual power to impress with the landscape and seascape. Almost invariably it gathers aspects of that power from the fact that it is allied to the most powerful of landscape elements for its setting. There are 63,000 breeding pairs of fulmars on St Kilda, widely distributed, but it is at the Gap that they celebrate their finest hour.

The third phenomenon of the Gap is that your seaward gaze is magnetised to the prospect of Boreray and its stoical storm-fending stacs, Stac Lee and Stac an Armin. Boreray surprises with its size, especially its height; the stacs with their abrupt ocean-challenge. All three are chameleons of their own micro-climate, making their own mists which shade and shadow their appearance with a grey pallour, a black menace; or in strong sun and in season Boreray is a vivid emerald green above the cliffs. Stac an Armin is forever gannet-white in every weather, but even that stark shade glistens or dulls as sun and cloud and storm make their plays.

Already you feel on the roof of an incredible world, with further horizons than you have ever known, but you are only halfway up Conachair. It has begun as gently as St Kilda permits.

Boreray's ". . . stoical storm-fending stacs, Stac Lee and Stac an Armin . . ."

At the Gap

All around, behind,
the tilt of land on
heather-hilted feet

had so conspired,
deceived, contrived
to lull unwittingly even

the second last stride.
The last tensed back
from Hirta's sudden brim where

the view springs
like a trap, snaps
shut on sensibilities.

Eyes stammer down
– a fulmar-strewn gasp,
beyond – Boreray

afloat in its dawn,
stac-serried,
bird-powdered.

Some old protective
mainland inhibition
lurched free then

and by its freedom
won St Kilda
another unshielded heart.

"... winds crush in a chaos of mad airs into the Dùn Passage, gralloching the rock ..."

YOU HAVE greeted the birds. You must now greet the rock and the sea.
There would be a time when Ruaival and Dùn were one, a sea-contemptuous rock-ridge, nature's unbreachable harbour wall. But time is the enemy here of everything but the sea, and in patient unwearying warring, the sea has first caved, then tunnelled, then collapsed, then split the promontory, prised the two apart with the water-wedge of the Dùn Passage.

At sea level, the two land masses are no more than a dozen yards apart, a perilous boulder-hopping crossing at low tide, but, it must be said, a crossing which simply strands most mortals at the foot of a grim rock wall. At their summits, Ruaival has retreated a hundred yards. The two points of view offer two insights into the nature of the victim of the sea's ponderous assault.

By mid-afternoon the sun bears down on the Dùn Passage from the south-west, illuminates briefly the green-walled cave floored by green-crazed seas. That cave is a new stake driven into the heart of the Dùn and hammered ever more lethally home by every passing tide. The place is the haunt of seals and eiders, and in the lit water you can watch the seals' every underwater gesture; the world has few clearer seas than this one.

It remains an uneasy, untranquil corner of St Kilda even in its rare hours of profound calm, and a place of some storm-spectacle. In a south-westerly, winds unhampered by anything this side of Ardnamurchan Point rush into its crazily sea-paved outer courtyard, crush in a chaos of mad airs into the Passage, gralloching the rock, gouging the Passage ever wider, ever deeper. The north face of Dùn confronts you from low on Ruaival, a prospect like the end of a hideously magnified bar of Toblerone.

The sea has accorded you one privilege here, for it has unwittingly laid bare for your scrutiny the inside of an island. We are a tribe of surface treaders. We plumb the depths of seas, but not lands, never rocks unless they harbour riches. Here, however, the sea offers this uncanny perspective, so that you sit and stare and trace veins and arteries, and shudder at the power of the torso.

It is nothing less than characteristic of St Kilda that for all the furies which mass at the west end of the Passage, the gentle flow of the Village Bay waters from the east so buffers the onslaught that the eiders lead their two-day-old chicks here, and take them fearlessly to these waters rather than dare the presence of man. You learn, doubtless, to take wildness in your stride when it is your first stride which tests it. A literal translation of the eider chicks' instinctive storm-relish must also have rubbed off on those St Kildans born into this landscape. Wildness is only awesome when it is not a way of life.

There is a sudden small stir in the bay, a rising sound, a soft cacophony of voices; a white-winging unstructured flock gathers at the mouth of the Passage, and moves in a loose-woven plaid through the channel, black rock for a backdrop, sun-spotted each individual bird, green-garnished the sea; all the waves and winds have taken the Passage all day from the west, but this bird-wave graces the place from east to west, climbs into the sun's undaunting glare. The sound echoes back from beyond the sun: "Kittiwake! Kittiwake!"

The summit of Ruaival peers down the dog-eared spine of Dùn, watches it trail seaward to the forlorn isolations of Levenish. It is a bumbling ridge, fractured and peaked, hacked and hewn by all manner of weathers, violent greens on the village side where its grasses, ungrazed in 50 years, grow knee-deep and spawn the burrowed offspring of 40,000 pairs of puffins.

A grey skyline bruise swells and rushes down on the island. Clouds clamp down on the Dùn, swither about the bay, then blot the crowns of Oiseval and Conachair. Ruaival survives but the world which has so commanded your eye for hours is suddenly denied to you, a suddenness which shocks. Your only line of vision is down, down to the Passage, down to the western sea, down to the bay where the kittiwake flock reassembles on the water, contriving to look both demure and morose at the same time. Winds hammer the rock, drag down the stinging rains, vent their ocean freedoms on this green blot on their seascape. The sheltering boats make a run for it round to Glen Bay, a familiar ritual for St Kilda seafarers. The mile back to the tent is as shelter-free as any mountain plateau. The storm rages an afternoon and a night, a formidable sustenance of raw energy, then melts to a new morning's blue breeze, a glistening island idyll in its wake. On such a day, the summit of Conachair, the summit of all St Kilda commands.

It is the first day for a month in which the horizon has hardened; the summit finally clears of its thirled mists; Boreray and its stacs, vivid with gannet-glitter, wear the air of bizarre craft afloat on the sea, the water so calm that there can surely be no island roots beneath. Land other than St Kilda's own is visible (a fact worthy of conversation itself hereabouts), a smirr of darker blue than the

Ruaival dips a shoulder into the calm waters of Village Bay

Shapes and summits
top left   *Soay glows green*
top right   *Oiseval's bloated pyramid*
bottom   *Dùn tilts energetically westward*

sea, the white-sanded Western Isles 40 miles to the east.

Strangely this rare glimpse of a far shore does not amount to the reassurance of worlds beyond, which you might expect, for if you have given yourself to the spirit of St Kilda's other-worldliness, you will see in that serrating of your horizon only an irrelevance, a far veiled threat of intrusion perhaps, but so far, so veiled, that it cannot seriously impinge.

Levenish, dourest of St Kilda's satellites, nurtures its own small storm. It is always dark on Levenish, the water always white, the birds always elsewhere, or so it seems. It is a drab, forlorn thing, ill-at-ease and hangdog amid the jewels. The Dùn, bold and erratically beautiful in any weather, tilts energetically westward, rock wings akimbo, daring the western ocean as ever, and being caught again and again from behind by a rare prolonged interlude of south-easterlies, so that the eternal sea-gnawing rubs salt into unaccustomed stone wounds. Soay is big and green and aglow.

We – the fulmars, the bonxies, the wrens, a speculative golden eagle from that forgotten eastern shore, and I – are at the centre of our universe, an oasis in a blue Sahara. The birds here are grace notes to the wild music of the place. Two peregrines on a far hill rebuke an unseen breach of their peace, their cries carrying a mile on the restless air. Two bonxies rise from their heather couch, orchid-patterned, to stand and point their wings skywards, quacking softly in the manner of unlikely ducks. It is a handsome, endearing gesture.

Snipe cries ricochet across the hill, not the mellow drumming of their high-diving flights but a stammering, stabbing, jabbering dirge, like a recording of hiccups.

It takes a wren to drown that out. Long after you learn not to be astonished at St Kilda's unlimited capacity to astonish, you will be astounded at the places you encounter wrens, at the free flow of sweet song, at its power to lift, however fleetingly, even the pervasive mood of hodden-grey gloom with which St Kilda frequently garbs itself for days at a time. On such a day as this, however, there is nothing to dispel, but the joysong is a heady embellishment. He sings from the topmost rock of the highest pinnacle of a 50-foot stac three-quarters of the way up Conachair's 1200-foot cliffs. In St Kilda's tumultuous landscape, wrens are nothing-daunted.

But any sweet song of wilderness on Conachair's summit is embittered by the jarring discord of Mullach Mór's tracking station, and the new radar station beyond. These are St Kilda's contribution to the defence of the realm, not that the realm was ever particularly mindful of St Kilda for much of its history, and the kindest sentiment you can afford them is that St Kilda shutters them in mist for much of their lives. On such a day as this, however, they are simply an affront. Their place, if they have one, is elsewhere, their presence a denial of the value of landscape. It is easy enough to turn your back on them and marvel at half the wild world; it is easy enough to walk beyond them and rush avidly down into the good green embrace of Gleann Mór's hills; but they lodge in your subconsciousness like a mild toothache which effects a discomfort far beyond the size and bodily significance of the tooth.

The fact of the stations has spawned all St Kilda's imperfections. For this of all landscapes, there should be a better way.

B UT NOW I have dropped Gleann Mór into this reckoning of landscapes, and with it a store of beauties. It is here in the north-west corner of Hirta that the heartbeat of St Kilda is a tangible pulse. The mad God's hoard has clustered its finest pieces here, and set bonxies to guard them, a role they perform diligently and, whiles, to excess.

The traverse of the island from Village Bay to Glen Bay – Loch a' Ghlinne – through Gleann Mór is an aged pilgrimage. As you climb to meet the inevitable mist skull caps on the island brows, you tread the path followed twice a day by the St Kildan women to milk the cattle in Gleann Mór and carry the milk back to Village Bay — sea level to 800 feet to sea level, and back; a formidable ritual. But it was done because it was done.

The road has formalised their path at least as far as the watersheds when it snakes up into the mists and technology's blurred thumbprint. The parting with it for "mountain mosses singing at your tread" in Argyll poetess Marion Campbell's phrase, is gladdened by a snatch of snow bunting song, a fruity, head-turning trill, a familiarity of many mainland winter summits (and a handful of summer ones), but the last voice in ornithology's Babel of tongues you would expect to carol at you from a St Kildan bog. You learn, as you grow accustomed to St Kilda's speech, to expect anything. All manner of fly-by-nights take what

The slopes of Conachair and the Army road to the installations on Mullach Mór

they can from St Kilda, grateful for its ocean isolation; that at least is not the exclusive preserve of humanity.

Cleits both mark the path and mislead it by blurring off on every side, a ragged hunchback army in perpetual retreat before overwhelming elemental odds. Finally, the contour of an old turf dyke emerges, and as it drops from the watershed of Mullach Sgar, the mists relent, the wind is snuffed; before you sprawls a green round-hilled valley such as you never dared to contemplate in all your preconceptions of St Kilda.

Orchids thicken underfoot, butterworts star the damp places, roseroot fattens the rocks of the Abhainn a' Ghlinne Mhóir and shelters late primroses, but the perceived idyll splinters at the first downbeat of bonxie wings about your head, shatters at the second.

Bonxies – great skuas in ornithological parlance, but the more expletively appropriate "bonxies" to those who have suffered their bully-boy attentions – are a kind of missing link species, something between the biggest gulls and buzzards perhaps. Webbed feet the size of small paddles, a hooked beak which tears prey like puffins to shreds, a head-on way with humans who infringe territorial rights — these are bonxie characteristics. Fearlessness and powers and strength of flight in pursuit of another bird's catch are quite up to dispossessing an osprey or drowning a gannet. They are dark, awesome, sinister, handsome, majestic birds. Watching someone else being bonxied from a comfortable distance is St Kilda's ultimate spectator sport.

Gleann Mór, like St Kilda itself, is not easily won, but the rewards repay the suffering. The high ground of Leathad a' Ghlinne is bonxie-freest, and from its relative calm the glasses catch the glint of a far lochan near the mouth of the glen. It has at first glance the air of a candle a-flutter with brown moths, but the moths are bonxies, the lochan the one tiny fresh watersheet in all St Kilda, the bonxies' vital bathing pool. It is justifiably off-limits in spring and summer months, but the spectacle of thirty or forty bonxies bathing and preening and drying off is riveting birdwatching, even from this peaceable distance.

A demure, aloof alien in their midst, chestnut-scarfed, is a phalarope. Five tufted duck gather there too, a foolhardy rendezvous considering how it is with bonxies and easy prey a quarter of their size. Perhaps the tufties have some foul-tasting immunity. Perhaps they are passing through and simply don't know

Gleann Mór: "It is here that the heartbeat of St Kilda is a tangible pulse . . ."

about bonxies. Two days later, there is one duck on the pond. The meadow pipits which spring before your tread from nests of wicker grass weavings must have a grim time of it. To think they thought their troubles were over because there are no cuckoos here . . . bird theorising on St Kilda is a good pastime, even if its base is not always overtly scientific.

To sit high above Gleann Mór, to contemplate the littering evidence of settlement, to populate its fertility with the shades of the earliest St Kildans (apart from one dark hint at An Lag above Village Bay, the oldest built remnants of St Kilda are here in Gleann Mór) is to induce a curiously saddening frame of mind. There is a melancholy element about any dishevelled remnants of old tribal tongues whose threads of speech have long been cut. The ancient patience of these stones has gone unrewarded, so that our best reconstructions are left to chancy guesswork.

Whatever the nature and number of Gleann Mór's earliest settlers, it must have been a beautiful if arduous existence. Today's glen enshrines the beauty intact, harbours none of Village Bay's civilising influences, whether the formalising of the 19th century street or the jarring grimaces of recent decades. There must be days of bonxie-free winter here when the stillnesses and the silences of the place are unbearably, achingly exquisite. It is to here of all St Kilda's landscape wonders that the mind's eye returns again and again: the high contouring walks along the Leathad a' Ghlinne; the burn-hugging dawdles, surprising a velvet scoter in a pool beneath a waterfall; the high reverberations of evening snipe; the long, haphazard ruminatings amid the shielings on old, old landfalls; anxious eyes hustling dark, nervous sheep up treacherous rocks; the first uneasy nights in crude shelter; the slow realisations of the richness of discovery . . . to have stravaiged seas such as these then stumbled on Gleann Mór must have seemed a rich reward from some nomad's God-of-the-Wilds.

The north sky clears, horizons harden far out beyond Glen Bay although the high ground of Mullach Sgar above the glen stays black, flings skittish showers the length of Gleann Mór. These catch fitful suns and shadows so that their progress down the glen is a pied dance, so that they smoke across Glen Bay in drab-and-dazzle stutters, so that the prows of the Cambir and Soay beyond shine and shutter in and out of turn. There is no trick of light which St Kilda finds impossible to work, no land-and-seascape device which is not in its

The Cambir and Soay from high in Gleann Mór: "It is to here of all St Kilda's landscape wonders that the mind's eye returns again and again . . ."

mesmerising repertoire. Nature's outlandish conjurer is always centrestage.

The east shore of Glen Bay so rivets your eyes on the vast caves and myriad crannies of the far shore and that two-prowed interplay of the Cambir and Soay, that its most startling showpieces are well shielded. Finally, however, as you reach the headland of Gob na h-Airde, your head will swivel seaward and on such a day St Kilda defies you not to exclaim aloud at the sight which greets you. At its centre is Boreray, or rather the site of Boreray, for only a protruding hint of its south-east shore is clear. A vast grey tree of mist, seemingly miles high, is rooted deep into Boreray's spine, spills impenetrable foliage down the island's flanks, relents only around the stacs, where branches wither and fall and rematerialise in unbroken sequences so that the stacs move in a dream-dance in and out of arches and tunnels of mists. For a moment the gannet-white south flank of Stac Lee catches stray sunlight, flares like a candle in wind then gutters out in another obliteration of mists, so that you blink and try frantically to reconstruct the instant. The futility of that idea is compounded by the knowledge that by lingering over St Kilda's last trick, you will miss the next. You let it go, and hope that retrospection will safeguard it for you.

You stand now on the flank of a tiny bay fashioned from 200-foot cliffs, tiny by St Kilda's standards, and unimpressive only if you permit your gaze to rise up and up to Conachair's monstrous northern profile. Kittiwakes drift through the bay like stray snowflakes, but the bay is the setting for another of St Kilda's bird climates in which one species so pervades the cliffs and the water, and the airspaces and flightpaths between, that the land and seascape seem to have colonised the birds, rather than the other way round. A long horizontal crack runs the length of the bay's east cliff, perhaps a hundred yards, with a second storey crack above its seaward end. Into its sunless embrace are crushed so many guillemots that in their densest groupings it becomes impossible to identify individuals. More and more fly in every second so that the perpetual impression is of a cliff with the properties of blotting paper. There is no such thing as too many guillemots. The ones which find their chosen landing space saturated have the ability to cling to the guano-painted frieze beneath while the pack above reshuffles enough to permit one more.

To follow the flightpath of a single bird from cliff to sea and ultimately back to the same predetermined unsquare inch of cliff is a revealing study of the nature

top   *The headland of Gob na h-Airde*
bottom   *Boreray and its foliage of mists*

The Tunnel: "... St Kilda's ultimate wonder..."

of seabird politics, although understanding it all would take a little longer. Say a lifetime.

But this small headland, having bruised you with bonxies, staggered you with Boreray and its mists, enthralled you with its guillemot city and its panorama of Glen Bay, has still not finished with your sensibilities. Its ultimate treasure, St Kilda's ultimate wonder, lies beneath your feet as you cross back to the Glen Bay side. A gentle rock scramble down through nesting fulmars and posing razorbills gives way to a wide rocky ramp down the cliff-face (and inclining mercifully towards it and away from the drop to the sea) to what looks at first sight to be the mouth of a vast cave. You may have learned by now, however, that nothing in St Kilda is so unreliable as a first glance and that, accordingly, the cave is not a cave. The ramp widens as it dips towards the sea, and you reach thankfully for a rope which enables you to cling to the cliff-side despite the underfoot treacheries of sea and rain drenched rock. Haltingly, you ginger into the Geò na h-Airde, otherwise known as the Tunnel. There are many tunnelled headlands on St Kilda, from crouching-canoeist dimensions upwards, but nothing comes close to this for its scale and its spectacle.

The Tunnel, like the Gap, is one of those St Kilda phenomena about which seasoned voyagers will warn you and, like the Gap, the warnings merely fashion trivial preconceptions for the reality to obliterate.

The Tunnel is huge. It is also dark and cold although light and warmth flood both ends. The rocks slip warily down from the rope to the sea's carved channel in the tunnel floor, a tremulous place of head-on tides propelled into a chaotic meeting by the seas on both sides of the headland. In storm, the spectacle is a rock-shuddering sensation beloved of Glen Bay's seals. On becalmed days, the channel is never still, the water at its heart forever white, forever restless on its yielding rock. The underwater play of seals is as patently watchable as their surface frolics, but your eye is dragged away again and again to the walls and roof of the amphitheatre, until you venture deep enough into the tunnel for its eastern mouth to frame Boreray in one more head-spinning setting. From the heart of the Tunnel that aperture assumes the shape of a map of Africa, with Boreray lodged somewhere about Zaire.

The seas rush vividly in, collide, confuse, concede, succumb to the next rush, the rushing and colliding amplified and reamplified by limitless echoing of the rock chamber. Kittiwakes cry in the Glen Bay mouth, the guillemot colony of the two-storey crack blurs about the far end. Seals tail-stand and eyeball your ungainly crabwise descent, then infinitely surer of their own fractious element, slip down and down into the visible depths, then spiral back to stand and stare again. Preposterously in all this voluminous sorcery, a wren sings, and pours the huge gentility of its echoed song over every rock and wave and watching ear. The sound and the scene fuse. They will stand memory's test a lifetime.

It is a dazed climb which evacuates the Tunnel, concedes that it is the environment of seals and seas and wrens and trembling rocks and phantom Africas. There are other forces at work here too, less definable things which run deep, infiltrate rock portals and prey on susceptible minds. You have no word for them, but many thoughts; no response, but a spiritual gratitude for what they may have awakened.

It occurred then that the Passage at Dùn was roofed in like this once, that you wandered from Ruaival to Gob an Dùin with the sea and seals and probably the wrens in turmoil far beneath your tread. So what is at work in the Tunnel is the severing of one more headland into one more stac, a perpetual surgery whose only ultimate outcome is amputation. It will be a great loss when the roof falls in, for there is nothing in the landscape of skies to match this vault, nothing so airy as the confines of this great ocean's burrow. The might of the ocean will be dispelled by the execution of its mightiest gesture, but by that time there will doubtless be other tunnels.

You surface again to find Boreray adrift of its mists, the horizon a hard blue crayoned line across the world, Stac Lee's candle boldly lit, an idle ambling sea about their ocean midst; Gleann Mór a vivid summer green; Glen Bay awash with eider-and-seal-croon, a lush lather of sound. The winds have wandered elsewhere, the skull caps of Conachair and Mullach Mór doffed to the sun; St Kilda basks. The peace which washes over Gleann Mór and its old untold stone stories is a long, lingering sigh. Beautiful and peaceful are not the words for it. Some unfashioned superlative which fuses both and layers the land with the accumulated spirits of great age — such a word might fit.

So now you must shoulder the milk of Loch a' Ghlinne and Gleann Mór, and bear that burden back across the watershed to the road and the village and its strolling players, the small bustle of vehicles and boats and the order of the

Sentries of the shore: an immaculately turned out quartet of razorbills

48

society which has gone and the one which has replaced it less confidently. It seems a strange argument to protest the presence of civilisations on somewhere like St Kilda, but landscape forces still predominate here, and once you have tasted the single malt of landscapes, your appetite for the blends dwindles. After Loch a' Ghlinne, Village Bay will always be a blend, albeit one of many subtleties and finer qualities as well as flaws and frailties.

As you climb Gleann Mór, you fall to wondering in this wonder-filled place about those first St Kildans again, about their choice of this glen rather than the easier and deeper-sheltered option of Village Glen. Was it a decision of defence, of the suitability of land for sheep and cattle, perhaps even of a judgement on landscape? It is a touching if fanciful theory to contemplate that the settlement's overriding consideration was simply the beauty of the surroundings, perhaps a spirituality fuelled by landscape?

The bonxies accord short shrift to such flights of unfounded and unfoundable philosophy, for the strides between territories grow shorter year by year, and now the entire glen is a procession of much vigilance. Aircraft wreckage litters a hillside high on Gleann Mór's western flank, and it is a short mental stride from encounters with pieces of wing and fuselage to the idea of bonxies queueing up in the sun . . . "Bandits at four o'clock . . . " and the ensuing strafing run at unwary heads.

You rejoin the road by the pillar box and the bus stop and the zebra crossing – civilising St Kilda has not been without humour – and try in your mind's eye to isolate the village and its attendant maze of dykes from the rest, the better to bear home the Gleann Mór milk. It is not impossible, this willing self-deception, and serves at least to heighten the fascination of once-upon-a-times, to ponder the rigours of that milk-fetching ritual and the many others which must have been a matter of routine, and to ponder whether the women who were its beasts of burden blessed Gleann Mór as you had just done for the effect of its beauties on lightening the load, or cursed it for its bogs and hills. Would they cherish its landscape knowing no other, as most of us do today who have seen nothing like it? Did some of them long, in the darkening demise of Village Bay, to cross the hill and start again, afresh, in the instinctive land of their predecessors around Loch a' Ghlinne? They are futile lines of thought, but they intrigue, simply because again and again they occur.

right   *Conachair draws a discreet veil over the Village*
far right   *". . . inevitable mist skull caps on the island brows . . ."*

Conachair in Mist

Hirta wears
her hodden, sodden greys
as handsomely
as any of her shades,
her hill-spun monochromes
as fine, as fitting as
any glad-ragged summer.

Leeching mists
rain cleits on Conachair.
These huddle tidily
like thoughtfully exploded screes
and fingerprint the hill
with cloaked identities
of Hirta's hodden tribe.

MIDNIGHT. Thick, flat clouds have layered darkly above the western horizon, or at least as darkly as it will get, a murky half-light. In the north, the sky already pales, but the clouds are vital. It is the perfect night for one of St Kilda's eerier ornithological adventures. The path winds intermittently down 600 feet of a cliff face you would probably rather not contemplate in broad daylight, or even a cloudless moonlit night. Immense rock shapes begin to gather round. Unexplained bird scufflings suggest that the natives are restless at such thoughtless intrusion into their brief hours of dark security.

The intruders – six members of the Royal Air Force Ornithological Society, the NTS/NCC warden, and the scribbler – scramble off into an ankle-wrenching boulderfield 300 feet above the sea. The place is a treachery of clefts and holes and hollows and overhangs and underhangs shot through the feet and heads of boulders the size of a doorstep or the size of a house. Such a place is Carn Mór, the collapsed seaward flank of Mullach Bi, summit of St Kilda's west coast. It is also home to a bizarre trilogy of night-homing birds: the Manx shearwater, Leach's petrel and the stormy petrel.

In the long hour which follows, you find what comfort you can in a midnight boulderfield. The chat sparkles, the prize of convivial company; fulmars bicker restlessly, oystercatchers complain the way they do, even when they are blatantly enjoying themselves; far below, the ocean flicks a 15-foot swell at the base of the tormented cliff.

Tea, whisky, soup, whatever, eases the wait. A small underfoot fury – disgruntled puffin – clatters for the sea, to be followed by a faintly hysterical chuckle and a swallowy silhouette about our heads, the first Leach's petrel. Thirty frustrating minutes later there is the first shiver, and then the second giggle, then all giggling hell breaks loose. Birds flicker bat-like, inches away, at what appears in the gloom to be something akin to flat-out swallow speed; the air rings to the chuckles, and the rocks answer – the response of burrowed birds to the homecomers – with muffled variations on the same theme. The pattern of notes is almost invariably the same, but the pitch varies widely from soothing contralto to Yingtong Song farce.

They cackle round like firecrackers, their shouts dancing off the rocks in every direction, until suddenly, after an hour of the nonsense, one answers the invasion from somewhere below and between your legs! You have been sitting

". . . the collapsed seaward flank of Mullach Bi's coast . . ."

for two hours on a petrel burrow. The hand tape recorder which has been patiently whirring in hope at the dark now catches the sound. By replaying it at the mouth of the burrow, the bird within begins to respond to its own voice. It may be cheating, but there was a curious elation in the act of being able to coax one of our rarest seabirds to sing, almost at will.

A new note — the Manx shearwater's bronchial wheeze, a four-syllable gentle banshee which the bird books tell you sounds like "avocado". With a liberal imagination and the concession of an unlikely emphasis on the "ca" syllable, avocado is no more of an absurdity than the symphony which now begins to unfold. The giggling is unrelenting, the wheezing a rhythmic underpinning with a tendency to end as if something was going to be sick, which is possibly the consequence of too much avocado. When the rude, snoring bass of the stormy petrels finally intones somewhere around 2.30, its bizarre score is complete, the symphony finished.

You have been in the throes of privilege, for that is what it is to share the intimacy of the wildest rituals in nature, to have the rarest and most furtive of creatures flop about your feet and graze your shoulders and bounce in your lap, to summon them to song. They are graceless in their landings, these birds, and use the darkness to mask their shortcomings from the big gulls and the bonxies. They simply hit land, and stagger dazedly amid the rocks until the right call emerges from the right burrow, and the waiting birds can change places with the homecomers.

It is a primitive affair at which to be present, made all the more memorable by the fact that it relies for its effect on sensation and sound rather than sight. Stunned birds can be calmly handled by experienced knowing hands for a few seconds, but mostly the birds are shapes and shadows. It is the wildness of it all which lingers still.

By 3.00, most of the birds are in. The climb up Carn Mór is a tentative stiff-legged journey, but at every other stride there is a giggle or a wheeze or a snore to stop your tracks or crease one more smile. By 3.30, the dawn is a thing of snipe-scrolled beauty, augmented by wrens, pipits, oystercatchers, fulmars and the rest. It is not the dawn chorus of oakwood or lochside, for it is an altogether wilder more elemental thing of a wilder, more elemental landscape than anything which ever dawned on you before. It is, of all things, of its place.

"... the dawn is a thing of snipe-scrolled beauty ..."

59

left *Fulmars slice sleekly through the air above Aird Uachdarachd; Boreray crouches beyond*

above *A single bird with roosting notions in the last of the sun*

It is 4.00, the tent greeted stiffly, the daylight now bright, the fulmars in full throat, the wrens cheerfully vibrant, the petrels and the shearwaters half an island away. The prospect of a few hours sleep and a late rise appeals, but there have been other burrowers abroad in the night. Inside the tent, a half-eaten Bounty bar lies in the middle of the sleeping bag. Six apples out of eight have been violated by small teeth and small droppings, and a packet of soup has been scattered far wider than you would ever have believed possible. Two holes the size of ten pence pieces have been drilled into the floor and the wall of the inner tent — St Kilda's unique fieldmouse has performed a unique disservice. There are moments, even on St Kilda, when proximity to wildlife is less than a blessing. You cannot pick and choose friends and foes in wildlife, of course; you wished them no harm, but if they come back, perhaps they would care to chew instead on this box of matches.

It is 5.00. Sleep in the tidied tent (with improvised deterrents to ward off any return by the same entrance) is tortured by oystercatchers and fulmars and fitful dreams of internally combusting St Kilda mice. For what remains of this early morning, only the stormies are snoring.

CARN MOR from above and in brilliant noon light is a bird sanctuary of a different feather. It proves to be little more than a subsidiary prow of Mullach Bi, but suffers only in comparison with the thrusting seaward bowsprit which culminates in Sgeir Mhór. From Mullach Bi's summit at almost 1200 feet, these tumbledowns of disintegrated cliffs crash seaward in a monstrous chaos of rock. It is as though a primeval landslide had been frozen by some vindictive force determined to thwart its eager turmoil for the sea. Huge rocks perch unconvincingly on mere boulders, while seas rehearse their jowls far below. It is a terrain which makes more demands on the mind than it does on the physique.

At noon there is no hint of the night's bird commotions. Fulmars attend, of course, rebuke and unnerve with their flypasts, and desultory puffins clockwork brightly by; starlings scratch and wrens sing and sing, but there are no snores, no giggles, no avocados.

Mullach Bi is an arrogant jaw of a summit, a place of frantic winds, a place to befriend a boulder and consider the whole of Hirta's west coast from Soay to the

Dùn, while over your shoulder the riches of Gleann Mór fold down and down in their green serenity. Is there a single summit which straddles such chalk-and-cheese landscapes as these, anywhere in the land? You scour the landscapes of your mind and find none.

The Dùn from here is a landscape rag, a frayed stray of a thing, a shed leaf which has bowed half a world of oceans before its wind and lodged untenably on some toehold of Ruaival, clung tremblingly there while the wind relented. Ruaival itself, that eyrie of such imposing dominance above the village, above the Passage, is a small apprentice now, humbled by cloth cap mists which are donned and doffed with due respect to every flung shower. The Dùn wears these too, but jauntily on its many skulls, and lets them slither seaward like scarves, till the next whip of wind stings them into the ultimate submission of all sea mists. Conachair and the rest just mourn all day, hills in a shroud, the still centre of an island-wide whirlpool, the unblinking eye of its storm. These are the best of all St Kilda's days when suns and fast skies compete to shine and shade the land so that it is never undappled, so that the air is never still, so that the sea-glitter shifts like a tapped kaleidoscope, so that the helter-skelter perspectives of the dwindling southward cliffs are confused by ever-fluctuating light which defies the focus of your eye. Yet in such landscape fervours, Conachair and Oiseval and Mullach Mór hold their high brotherhood aloof, decline the festivities.

Soay also catches their mood, but restlessly, so that though its mists never win free, they tear before the wind's blade, or pierce at the sun's lance, then heal their own wounds only to scar again and again. The walk from Mullach Bi to the Cambir in the far north-west of Hirta is a coast-walker's Christmas, luring you continually to one more gasp over the rim of the western cliffs and their tantalising seas, demanding your gaze revert to the round-hilled sweeps of Gleann Mór. It is a disconcerting juxtaposition, eerily laced by the cries of skulking whimbrel. There are none of the curlew-cousin's graces to these birds; they are hunched, hapless, tuneless beasts with only their uncompromising wildness to recommend them, and the fact that they choose to live here.

The coast swoops down 800 feet to the narrows of the Cambir, then climbs and fattens to its last green outpost 600 feet above the sea — straight above the sea. The Cambir is another of those St Kildan outposts which harbour ensnaring moods, so that you can come upon the headland in any frame of mind you care

"Mullach Bi is an arrogant jaw of a summit, a place of frantic winds . . ."

to name, but if you will sit and still and submit, the power of landscape will overwhelm it. In its place you may become aware again of that same wilderness sense of profound privilege — that you coincided with that specific set of circumstances of lighting and weather and storm or sanctuary, and saw them make their play. It is something of which Colin Baxter has also spoken publicly and he has more cause to know it than most, for even in the wildest of landscapes he seeks out the quietest hours of dawns and dusks when the privilege of ultimate wildness is often won. That the landscape repays such a sensitivity to its subtleties is proven in these pages.

You sit then on the top landing of a collapsed vertical staircase of crazy paving long overgrown with vivid green whorls of turf. Nothing two-footed ventures here unless it also has wings. Across a narrow sound, Soay looms 600 feet higher and offers its widest bulk. If your imagination runs to considering a map of Soay as a slightly deformed horse with a head almost as big as its body, then the Cambir contemplates its nostrils, but also every yard of its silhouette from the tip of its ears to its forefeet. Whether you dare to deliberate on sea-horses three-quarters of a mile high or not, the proximity of its misted bulk confers a certain vulnerability on the Cambir.

Your first glance down the staircase to the sea reveals two unsuspected stacs and, although the map says "there they are" and confers 240 feet on Stac Biorach and 200 on Soay Stac, there is nothing in that two-dimensional scheme of things to accord them the presence they possess in reality. Stac Biorach is a gem, a cooling-tower shaped rock with a dished crown which at first glance looks like a badly chequered tablecloth. The glass unravels the riddle — the place is awash with razorbills and guillemots, the rock summit intensely whitened by guano, and flecked black and whiter white by the seething mass of their toings and froings and we-will-not-be-moved resistances to every other toing and froing.

Soay Stac is comparatively birdless, although puffins gather in half-hearted numbers on its more accessible corners, and there are few enough of these. It runs in a skinny Cuillin-ish ridge from just under the foot of the Cambir almost to Stac Biorach. That astonishing little spine apart, the stac is also pierced by the sea, and on such a day of winds, and wild sun-shot colourings, there is a perpetual riveting drama beneath your feet of which it is impossible to tire. Sometimes you feel you should applaud. Another day you will climb to the

"The coast swoops down 800 feet to the narrows of the Cambir . . . then climbs to its last green outpost . . ."

65

Soay at Dusk

And would the old stone-dwellers of Loch a' Ghlinne
scale the Cambir to pilfer sunsets,
store them in memory's cleits?

Or had such suns no power to free minds
so yolked to lands?

And how many suns have Turnered Soay's
amphitheatrical skies before and since, their
exhibited art unscrutinised, their brushstrokes
unremarked by the blinded eyes and turned backs of
extinctions and evacuations?

When our own momentary witness engraves
one sky, one ocean, one island
with one sun's scribbling summer finger, we acknowledge
suns which lit the volcanic birth and arced
across the island's prime, until
in its sea-crippled death throes
St Kilda prepared for 4000 years of man.

*Stac Biorach (**left**) and Soay Stac (**above**): "... two miniatures of the mad God's hoard ..."*

Cambir in eager anticipation of an encore, and find even these stacs shuttered in mists so that if this had been your first, perhaps your only visit, these two miniatures of the mad God's hoard would have hugged their jewellery to themselves. Such is St Kilda.

There is a third stac here, a humble unpretentious thing like one of Monet's haystacks with seemingly nothing to recommend it until your dawdling eye chances on a white slavering shock of water running thinly down from its pointed crown to the sea. The glass identifies a black crack down the face of the rock, the only clue that the stac is split right through. With every other shuddering swell, the sea tongues flicker in and carve away one more tiny flaw of rock. Stac Dona will soon be two stacs, and the sea will have claimed another victim. It is strange how, with all of Soay widespread before you, it is an effortless two hours you can spend ignoring it completely, but eventually you come back to its wild giant bulk.

The map recognises no contour lower than 400 feet, which is a tribute to its awesome shores. It is a brooding place of many wildnesses, rarely visited now, ruled by nature's own harsh regime. It matters that a place like St Kilda exists, and that within it there should be places left to their own devices, wild for their own sake. Soay still has its sheep and these exert a relict influence from the long-dead St Kildan heydays, but they flourish or fail now by nature's shepherdings, as wild as the laws to which they adhere. The sheep apart, Soay is unregulated wilderness, untampered, untrampled, undisturbed. It is simply there and from the simplicity of that fact derives great comfort. You know no compulsion to dare its cliffs and set foot on Soay. The fact that it is there is enough. There is much the puffins will know of Soay which is beyond our reach, and that is as it should be.

From Ruaival with its end-on island, Dùn, by way of Carn Mór and Mullach Bi to the Cambir with its head-on island, Soay, is as distinguished, as memorable an assembly of rocks and contours and seas as you will encounter anywhere. Not anywhere on St Kilda, just anywhere. You cannot tramp such a coast and feel indifferent, or emerge from the experience anything other than a gladder and a wiser man. If you can now sail it, having tramped, you will win something deep in the understanding of St Kilda's landscape.

THOSE THREE essential elements of St Kilda, rock, sea and seabirds, coincide and collide nowhere more forcefully than Boreray and its stacs – Stac Lee and Stac an Armin – and all their rocky hangers-on. There are a quarter of the world's gannets here, and on occasions it feels as if there are a quarter of the world's seas as well. From a small yacht the ocean brims, the crumpled waters of the swell obliterate horizons in the troughs, the islands rise and fall at the most bizarre of angles, and subtly shift positions as you wend the four mile passage from Hirta.

First, however, you linger under Oiseval and Conachair, the better to comprehend the landscape bluff that is St Kilda. Oiseval is the principal conspirator in it all, for where from Village Bay it deceives as a meekly round-flanked hill, the sea unmasks it for a pyramid, one side of which has been blown out into a long curve like a vast mainsail. Oiseval has a unique place in your affections among St Kilda's summits, of which more later, but as so often happens on St Kilda, the sea voyage offers a radically different interpretation on a piece of ground you thought you had come to know well.

Sailing in under the Gap towards Conachair you come finally face to face with the highest cliffs in the land from below, and for all the evidence you have seen with your own eyes all over St Kilda, Conachair from the sea looks an unassailable bastion.

Yet even as the thought conceives, even as your climbing eye confirms it, the light shifts to catch the throats of caves you could sail into. These swallow tide after angry tide, the anguish of their regurgitations resounding from deep inside the hill, and with every swallowing and every regurgitating, a little more of the bastion is breached. The patience of the sea is insurmountable — St Kilda preaches that at you day in day out, and it is an overwhelming truth. The fulmars, so dizzying in their flights from the Gap and so all-pervasive in that high foreground, are set now in a scale which reduces them to accessories. A second viewpoint always repays the effort on St Kilda.

It is a dark place, the bowels of Conachair. Shags, guillemots and razorbills gather on the ledges, and the rocks ring with all their concerted cacophonies and with the limitless song of the sea. You begin – but only begin – from such a position as this, to appreciate the skills of the cragsman who wagered life itself on his intimacy with cliffs like these so that his tribe might live through one

"First, you linger under Conachair, the better to comprehend the landscape bluff which is St Kilda . . ."

*The gannet-rich cliffs of Stac Lee (**top**) and Boreray (**bottom**): "It is around Boreray that the cragsman was at his stupendous best . . ."*

more winter. As a workaday ritual of daily life, however, it confounds any efforts at reasoning. There is nothing in your experience of life to approximate to such a recurring matter-of-fact ordeal, no known points of reference which render the St Kildan's instinctive way with a rock face accessible.

The more you try to grasp at his mind, the better to put the cragsman's art in its island perspective, the more unsure you become of that which you thought you had begun to comprehend. It is an elusive enlightenment you seek, and with the conceding of its elusiveness you consign it to the back of your mind and put about for Boreray. It will not lodge there willingly for long, however, because it is around Boreray that the cragsman was at his stupendous best.

As you cross the four Atlantic miles to Boreray, the prospect over your shoulder slowly assumes another of St Kilda's deceptions: that of a calm, benign green place, a pastoral dream, just such a seduction as might have lured these first seafaring shepherds and their flocks 4000 years ago. You have to remind yourself of what you have just seen under the cliffs. Those foundation stones of Conachair were not a green place. This is a characteristic of St Kilda, that it creates so profoundly and with such startling suddenness a succession of landscape moods; each one so convincing that it can obliterate the memory of the one before, until the mood changes again and the mind adapts to the new circumstances as if there had been no other. On a travelling day, you might encounter a dozen new moods; on a resting day, perhaps only half that number. In a midwinter weariness, perhaps only one that lasts a week.

Now the deceptions begin to work in reverse so that Boreray, for so long demurely green on its horizon, sheds that cloak and bares her darkly cliff-sentried shores; she bares bulk too, and height, and you grasp then, with a confirming glance at the map, that the island is almost as high as Conachair and twice as formidable as a result.

The sea works feverish aggravations on Boreray; the rock piles into the most violent serrations and skylines, and if you catch them on a day of mists and flat calm (or at least as flat a calm as St Kilda can contrive), they wear a House of Hammer aspect. It says much for this singular landscape that even on a high summer moment of unrelenting blueness and chocolate box sparkles on the water, the abiding impression you bring back ashore is that you have been to a black place.

Behind Boreray

It is black behind Boreray
and small. All

suns dance darkly, throw
no shadows on rock
this black. Stac

Lee is a black berg,
its sunk seven-eighths beyond
the scope of suns
and me. We

who wave our puny daring
under Stac an Armin
creep tinily by.

You have also been to the Mecca of gannets. You win your first knowledge of their impact as Stac Lee passes distantly on your port bow (another element in the great St Kilda bluff — for all the broken nose bluntness which it thrusts at Hirta, it proves from east or west to have no bulk at all, a rearing wafer of rock). The glasses put the detail on Stac Lee's reputation. Gannets attend its summit and its waters and its airs like flies on a rotting carcase, but the whole truth dawns only once you have rounded the east shore of Boreray.

There comes a moment under that most daunting of shores as you round its north-east corner that Stac an Armin hoves mesmerisingly into sight; tall, black, raked at an uncanny angle, a jaunty witch's hat, but so close now that its true scale is an almost physical shock. Its summit leers down 644 feet at the sea, and it wears like an Everest snow plume a high-flown streamer of gannets. There is a brief respite while you take this in, your eye lunging from the stac to Boreray's bizarre northern Rockies, to sundry scattered lesser rock mortals of a mere hundred feet or so. Stac Lee emerges too, a mile and more distant, and for the next hour you succumb to the fascinations of the relationship between these two stacs, the presences they possess, the auras they emit, their powers to humble and diminish the meagre dimensions of one human form in their immense midst.

What concludes the respite is that the gannets suddenly lose their nerve and come at you in shoals. Something like 50,000 nesting pairs and uncounted thousands of hangers-on are gathered here, and as you try to penetrate the mass of birds which has now gathered above the boat to pin-point its highest fliers, your mind lurches back to the first encounter with the fulmars of the Gap. There the birds spiralled down and down so that the nearest to the sea were indecipherable bird-dust. Now you are cast in the role of dust, the birds spiral up and up, perhaps 1000 feet or, equally probably, much, much more. The sound and the sight and the smell of the world's oldest and largest gannetry amount to an experience to rival anything which might occur in a lifetime's explorations of the wildest places on earth.

It occurs then, fleetingly, illuminatingly, that here at least around Boreray and the stacs are fragments of wilderness. Here are lands and waters making their own rules and adapting to them, standing and falling by them, and that while the land exerts its rock-stubbornness in the face of the ocean, the finest accolade we wilderness-demeaning humans can accord their elemental existence is to

Stac an Armin, ". . . tall, black, raked at an uncanny angle, a jaunty witch's hat . . ."

allow it to proceed at its own untrammelled pace, in its own unfettered manner. To see it and to taste it is to know finally how much it matters.

Now it is Stac Lee which commands. Now at close quarters, and approaching it from the north, you see its bluff slowly unfold, see the flat-face bulk diminish, until due west of it, you are looking at rock more akin to the Inaccessible Pinnacle. The transfiguring is a fabulous rock wizardry, enhanced and intrigued inevitably by ocean light, and as you pass and sail south-west for Soay, you win back the familiar landscape friend of the view from the Gap. Stac an Armin, inevitably, dodges in and out of this limelight with thunder-stealer's indiscretions, and Boreray lords it massively over her formidable sentries.

The sail back should be an anti-climax, a let-down, a long unwinding trail home to set the store of treasures secure in your mind. Not just the treasures either, for you must populate that landscape for a while too with the St Kildans' pursuit of the gannets. That drags your mind back to the dilemma it encountered under Conachair, and the improbabilities of trawling for the bread of life on the cliffs of Boreray and the stacs only compound the dilemma and render more remote the understanding.

Yet perhaps that is as it should be. Their way of life is done, and while it lasted it was unique to them. Something of that exclusive heritage would diminish, even tarnish, if it was all instantly accessible to every passing tripper or curiosity-collector. Perhaps the understanding should die with the St Kildans. But these are retrospective thoughts gleaned long after the anchor dropped. The voyage itself leaves little time for philosophies to evolve, for St Kilda from the sea crowds sensations as thickly as gannets on Stac Lee, and the sprawled north coast of Hirta is before you now, with Soay and its silhouetted stacs to set against the receding Boreray. Soay's stacs have none of the grandeur of Boreray's, but they plug the gap of that narrow sound between Soay and the Cambir like the pillars of a blown-up bridge, which in a way is exactly what they are. Soon – soon, that is, by its own slow standards – the sea will turn the Cambir into one more.

But not even Soay concludes the serried highlights of the sail. The west coast of Hirta is a dream from a small boat on a fine day, as fitting a climax to any island sail as any wilderness God might devise. Mullach Bi glares down 1182 devastated feet of rocky chaos. You glare up and thank some power for the

Stac Lee at close quarters: ". . . you see its bluff slowly unfold . . ."

volcanic stillness which now prevails. Carn Mór extends the theme, and you ponder that rocky shambles in the new light of its bird secrets. Deep in its embrace, the petrels and shearwaters lie cool in the afternoon heat awaiting the freedoms which darkness will bring. Fulmars and puffins – and a wren, even at this distance, drowning sea-song – are Carn Mór's daylight themes. The fulmars swing down and thermal up the cliffs and buzz the boat, the puffins clown past and flock on the water riding the swell in their own loose rafts, burrowing beaks deep into their backs, in which position they could be just about anything.

The rock of An Torc slips blackly by, intriguingly translateable as either a castrated boar or, more likely under the circumstances, a whale.

White-watered commotions ahead signal the Dùn Passage, a glance through to Oiseval, then you linger down the sea flank of the Dùn itself which, if anything, is the most extraordinary sea-savaged piece of rock in the entire repertoire of these virtuoso islands. This close, and from below, some conception of the power of seas over lands this vulnerable begins to assert itself. Here is the first hand evidence and the wrecked fruits of all the sea's labours. Another arch, another headland, and you experience again the peculiar gratifying calm of Village Bay, but a calm tainted now with the sudden absence of the day's predominant theme. There are many charms in Village Bay, but the wilderness which is St Kilda is elsewhere.

Y OUR WANDERINGS have set the St Kildans in their island context, the islands in their ocean context; it is better to have that knowledge before you dwell on the Village, for however fascinating the St Kildan way of life may have been, however sad and unworthy its conclusion, however compulsive its story, it is a story which depends for its significance on its landscape. It is also a story which is nothing more than a fragment of the landscape's own story, as Village Bay is nothing more than a fragment of St Kilda.

The Village is, for all the attendant distractions and uneasiness of the Army presence, a fitting museum piece, a worthy archive. To claim any more for it is to misinterpret the National Trust for Scotland's intent or to award a higher significance to the buildings than they merit. The Trust is responsible for much thoughtful restoration work in the Village, the result of eager volunteer work

Sea-savaged rocks:
right *Stac Lee 'end-on'*
far right *An arch on the headland of Dùn*

parties who pay sweetly for the privilege of labouring for two weeks at a time on pointing, roofing, rebuilding or restoring cleits and generally keeping at bay the ravages of St Kilda's winters on built stone.

The five restored cottages serve, externally at least, to hint at how the street might once have looked, but there can never be any of the clutter of workaday civilisation in the streets and on the meadows below the Village, no coarse plough, no child's laugh, no argument, no loving, no sharing of spoils, no reasoning of community concerns.

So the Village is a museum, at best an echo, which in its more seductive half-lights of dusks and dawns offers receptive moments for the pursuit of once-upon-a-times. But even these are at best guesses, for unless you have lived on Fair Isle or Foula perhaps, or unless you are one of St Kilda's dwindling and scattered band of ageing survivors (or the child of one of these who learned the islands' ways at a mother's knee, a unique understanding), there are few frail straws to clutch.

Birds have moved in even here, so that it is wren song or starling scrape or fulmar speech or snipe stutter which falls on passing ears from old stone walls, not fiddle bow or poem chant. The schoolroom is a small timewarp where you might anticipate some handed-down significance to bridge the years, but when you are there, when you would sit among the ghosts and bare your mind of every stumbling block you know how to, what is handed down is the childlessness of your surroundings. In the real world, there is no such thing as a silent schoolroom.

Village Street begins its long westering curve here, passing first under Oiseval and a gathering of enclosures, high-walled and wonderfully wind-free, and showing the same resourcefulness in their stone-workings as the fanks of An Lag. At its highest point the wall flanking the street must reach 15 feet, but fitted so snugly into its hillside, that it is only four or five feet on the uphill side.

There is one other such wall in the Village, and it surrounds the graveyard. If there is revealing spoor of the St Kildans it lies here, in the fact that almost none of the stones are inscribed, and those which are are among the most recent, doubtless after acquiring the mainland fashion. There would be no need for names of course, for there was no-one to inform other than themselves, and who in a village that size would not know who was buried where? It is a symptom

far left   *The north-west of Hirta with Soay beyond*
left   *The Village: ". . . a fitting museum piece, a worthy archive . . ."*

83

perhaps of a degree of community closeness which we cannot comprehend, because it was fostered on mutual interest and the mutual co-operation on which individual and collective survival depended. There is nothing remotely approaching a suburb, no aloof houses up the hillside or across the hill. St Kilda was isolation enough.

Something of that may steal over you of an evening wandering amid the cleits and black houses and beehive houses of the Village, with the snipe drumming their spring anthems and the bay's ever-present kittiwakes wheeling and alighting and crying on the wind. You may take your thoughts with you to a certain roofless cottage to try and frame some definitive fragment of St Kilda in a glassless window, the better to underpin your questing vision. Instead the window of your choice frames the grey thoughtlessness of the Army power station; it is as elusive a quest to visualise life in St Kilda's good times as it is to come to terms with some of the things which have happened since.

It was the same irresistible quest, however, which framed something of the following:

ALASDAIR GILLIES was a Loch a' Ghlinne man, or at least that had always been his instinct for as far back as he could date it. He spoke, thought, dreamed of returning to the wellspring of the island and the islanders, of re-rooting and re-cultivating the old tree that it might branch again where its first seed was sown.

He talked thus through the long Village Bay winter. He would put a cottage on the headland where the sea tunnelled clear through and collided with its other self in mid-tunnel, so that his foundations would dance to its tune. That way, he reasoned, his home would not just be of the land, as all their homes were, but also of the sea, which all their homes shunned. It was not wise, he said, to shun the sea. It was the sea which lured the seabirds and it was the seabirds by which they lived and breathed. He would put cattle in Gleann Mór again as there once were, and stir the lazy place with life, such as it had once known.

The Parliament considered this carefully, for it was revolutionary within their own experience. At first their objections were trivial, unconsidered, instinctive excuses in the face of something which they were not quite sure they

Gob na h-Airde from Loch a' Ghlinne (Glen Bay)

84

understood. Alasdair Gillies deflected them easily.

You would miss the Parliaments, they said.

I will climb over every day, he said. Didn't the womenfolk climb over twice a day to milk the cattle and carry the milk back?

Your foundations will rot, they said, with the seas, but he pointed to cleits which stood in trembling of the sea, but stood well for all that. Besides, he reasoned that by the time the sea had won through the whole headland and his cottage had fallen with the other rocks in all their forms, he would long since have ceased to have any use of the place.

The villagers did not like that, the idea that their homes should be expendable if the sea so cared. Anyway, they said, you could not perform the poetry with no others around you. The village revered and relished its poetry and Alasdair was among the best of its poets.

Stac an Armin, he said, Stac Lee, Boreray, these were three lines of poetry in themselves, a muse in themselves; they would fill his window and guard the poet's spirit in Gleann Mór. They did not like that either, and protested that the poetry was of the people, not the land, although some conceded that was not a convincing argument.

Finally the Parliament objected that Alasdair Gillies was wrong in the pursuit of his dream, at which point he knew he had lost. The Parliament was never wrong, because the Parliament was the people themselves, and their decision was, by its own definition, the right one. There was no-one and nothing else to consider.

It was the creed to which they all clung, even Alasdair Gillies in his hour of dispute. The land, he pleaded, was before us, and will survive us. It moulds us and we respond to it by the manner of our building. The land does not respond to us, otherwise our fields would not reap such harvests of stones, otherwise our women would not bear dying children.

The Parliament said there could be no new house in Gleann Mór by Loch a' Ghlinne, because no sound case that they could understand had been made which would justify fracturing the community; poetry, which they cherished, was not in landscape; in fact they had no word for landscape.

Leave it, they told Alasdair Gillies. It is an old song, Gleann Mór, and it is sung. Stay with us and sing with us.

Village Bay and its hills: ". . . a stupendous sham, a masterly St Kildan deception . . ."

The Village

McDonald Gillies McQueen
the hearthstones still
commemorate evacuated lives
of 1930's husbands, wives

and children who returned
for tearful far-off Augusts.
The names mean nothing now: no cold tear
will resurrect St Kilda here.

No names can recompose
the hearthstone song
repopulate the long green street
or, treading lintels, meet

neighbours, kin, friends.
Yet from the shore
one wind-borne name occurs
and on those hearthstone names confers

a reminiscence for McQueens
and me and all our intervening years.
We bind with one freewheeling bond:
"Kittiwake! Kittiwake!" that wild St Kilda sound.

Then they offered the compromise. Build a cleit, they said. We need new cleits in Gleann Mór. Build it on the hill above the bay, and for as long as you take to build it, you may have your journeyings to the Parliament and your sea-stirrings and your poetry-in-land if it exists.

The decision was accepted, as all the Parliament's decisions were accepted, and with the good grace of all his tribe, but he had stirred unease with his ideas and vision and certainty and his talk of the land surviving the islanders, as if such a thing could happen. He hunched over his cleit, and hunched it in his own image against the seawind, but in his mind's eye it was a small, tight cottage, gable-on to the bay, with islands to set in his window and beneath his lintel. While he built, the sea throbbed in its tunnel, gnawing at the rock like a bonxie on a puffin. He built a good cleit, but because it was not his dream and not what he wanted to build, he did not go back to Loch a' Ghlinne.

When the time came – and he alone knew it would – to leave the island, he vowed privately he would be the first to go. He saw the seeds of decay, and found in the Parliament an inflexibility which encouraged the seeds. It was the land which mattered, and the sea, and being of the land and sea to the best of your ability. Given that, there was poetry and music, and without it, there was none. He would take his dream where it might be dreamed to the full . . .

. . . There never was an Alasdair Gillies on St Kilda, at least not that I know of, and not in that guise. He is my own half-wishful reincarnation, the symptom of my own feverish St Kilda madness, perhaps. Here of all places, the landscape has powers to move receptive minds to dream, and I fancy that had I been a St Kildan, I would have dreamed a house on a headland; I would have been a Loch a' Ghlinne man.

It is not an utterly futile exercise, because you cannot look at what was and what is and not dream it all a little differently so that the system – whether Britain's or St Kilda's own – might have permitted a little creative individuality for this individualistic place. The land has outlived the people; they only temper the poetry of the land now with the melancholy of their absence. The St Kildans found no way to evolve with the worst excesses of mainland tourism which adopted a zoo-like attitude towards its visitations; the mainland found no way to treat its discovery of St Kilda with the respect and unique consideration it deserved.

Cleits hunched against the sea mist

overleaf   *Stac a' Langa is dwarfed by Conachair's fulmar-strewn cliffs; Oiseval and Dùn flank Village Bay beyond*

Even now, when we like to think we have learned the worth of such consideration and respect, there is no recognition that (setting aside the larger consideration of whether or not the Army should be there at all) a substantial establishment of a quite alien nature to what exists should be housed with maximum discretion and care for the design of buildings. St Kilda's Army camp is a system-built one, by which I mean it is the only kind the system knows how to build. St Kilda is different enough and, as its World Heritage Site designation reflects, significant enough to warrant a more thoughtful solution.

The National Trust for Scotland, as landowners, have much to take pride in on St Kilda. It will never be an easy place to administer, and their policies do them credit here. In one sense at least, the work parties are the only people who are putting anything back into St Kilda, although it is too fleeting a contact to sustain any element of continuity. Even the Nature Conservancy Council's presence – which undertakes invaluable work – is often ill-at-ease and temporary. What St Kilda lost with its community was wisdom-through-age, and unless the Trust and its relationship with the Nature Conservancy Council ever establishes a year-round presence or some post-Army golden age ever seeks to re-establish a community on St Kilda, then it is lost forever. It is perhaps as well. Perhaps nature should have the freest reign human landowners can concede; she will have the last inevitable word in any case.

O ISEVAL steps steeply up from behind the tent, beginning with a boulderfield, studded on its higher slopes with dozens of cleits, so that from any distance its landward slopes have a clootie dumpling appearance. It is both the least spectacular and the most captivating of hills, for the way it works the backless-sideless trick, for its edge-of-the-world southern sky-line climb, for its small plateau summit which demands that you skirt it all the way round to win all its panoramas, for its backdoor familiarity to the tent-dweller. Here, by way of cementing our tentative bond, I spent my last St Kildan night. It is the best place to grasp the dimensions of Conachair, the best to dwell on the loneliness of Levenish, the best place to watch the evening light bewitch the Dùn across the bay.

With the light finally snuffed from Dùn, a contouring dawdle round the throat

of Oiseval meets the east coast just above the Gap. There is a faint flood of light still crossing the northern sky so that it glances obliquely on Boreray's west flank and tips the stacs. It produces an eerie trick of light which transforms Boreray into a monstrous hunchbacked creature of the prehistorics, its forelegs stout and short and bent like a tortoise, its spine the island's spine, declining to the tail of Creagan na Rubhaig Bana. The stacs stand sentry-stoical as ever. Fulmars wheel greyly by, and the wind which has whipped over the sea from the east all day is suddenly silent and spent. The stillness descends like a weight. Conachair has gone black, and Ruaival with it. The Dùn wears an impenetrable grey. Long after midnight, it is still light, the snipe still calling and drumming, the oystercatchers in the bay still shrilling. Boreray's monster dies with the light, resumes its island guise, so pale now it hardly seems a thing of substance at all, as if a decent breath of wind might bear the whole mass off into the night.

The reverse contour heads for the boulderfield, and the tent below. By two in the morning, the last conscious sounds are of a late snipe, and the early, wheezy "avocado! avocado!" of a homing shearwater. In the first moments of sleep, it sounds much more plausibly like "have a large one! have a large one . . . !"

T HE SCHOONER Jean de la Lune, my impromptu lift home, would make one last stop for its diving party behind Dùn. The talk was of the underwater world of shags and guillemots and seals, and I envied them that unseen side of St Kilda. I watched the land instead while they dived, watched the sea drive home minute after minute into the same cracks, holes, caves, tunnels; translated it mentally into an image of hour after hour, tide after tide, and marvelled again at the patient sculptures of its destruction, found gratitudes again at the privilege of bearing my brief witness.

She sailed then, a heady eight knots, while the Dùn folded softly into the darker embrace of Hirta, while the stacs sank lower and drowned, while all St Kilda shrank and paled over hours. Finally I followed the flight of a gannet with the glasses and when I returned them to the horizon it was unbroken. I fancied much later that I could vaguely re-assemble Boreray but fancy is what it was, or wishful thinking perhaps. No-one can re-assemble the St Kilda that was now that it has succumbed to its own horizon.

". . . the stacs sank lower and drowned, while all St Kilda shrank and paled . . ."

The Old Song

To have lived here
a hovel on Hirta
for your only hearth
(not nomads of science or soldiery
nor passing prowlers with pens
like me or Dr Johnson),
to bide all your times here
knowing no other's march
was to look wilderness in the eye
and dare it to deny
your daily bread.

To have lived here
content with all the world
in your embrace, at ease
with all its ways,
then hear compatriots whisper
"evacuate" was to feel
the soul's anchor drag,
to know that whatever the voyage,
wherever the final haven,
the journey was done,
the old song sung.